Chasing What Was

Cailey Parker

BookLeaf
Publishing

India | USA | UK

Presentation by *BookLeaf Publishing*

Web: www.bookleafpub.com

E-mail: info@bookleafpub.com

ISBN: 9789363304178

First edition 2024

inflation.

the greater the love, the greater the loss
the heavier the grief, the higher the cost

homesick.

t.s. elliot wrote
"home is where one starts from"
but i don't know if that's true
because losing you means starting over
but my home will always be you

unfinished.

the dust never settled
the sun never set
the flame never rekindled
the gambler never bet

meek me.

can't stand up for myself so i bend till i break
my confidence crumbles from all the chaos my
heart can't take

i wanna yell
i wanna scream

maybe the louder i am,
the more it will mean?
but i stay silent so i'm not *"too extreme"*

i shake
i shatter
only growing sadder
as i meet your needs
and forget mine ever mattered

rewritten.

i got lost and ended up in the wrong arms
but so did you
i toss and turn and get no sleep
because deep inside i know you knew
we'd come to an end
with everything left unsaid
tonight, are you in the right bed?

home is you.

you are my home base
you are my ground
you are where i feel safe
you are where i feel found

rosy perspective.

somewhere between strangers and friends
but still see you through a rose-colored lens

suffocating myself holding onto
yesteryear's regrets
and still afraid to confess that
with you, was as good as it gets

maybe we can pick up where we left off
if we just give it time
maybe someday i can make sense of
our story lingering so heavily in my mind

lesson in leaving.

been five damn years
i think it's time to face the truth
you're the one that got away
and i'm the one still hung up on you

i don't have any of your things to burn
cause it was just a fling to you
and i think that's what hurts
but i guess lessons learned always do

left on read.

everybody who ever loved him has lied
left him on read in real time with no reply
and those who said they'd be there
couldn't seem to find the time
when things got hard, they left him behind
family became few
friends fell off far and wide
but he didn't let that deter his mind
his heart was committed to staying kind
man, one like him is hard to find

selfless.

sweetest soul you'll ever meet
drowning in darkness you wouldn't believe
at war with anxiety, depression, and grief
so he stays detached to avoid defeat
while saving others
from the demons he himself can't beat

sobering silence.

new love
we both have found
but lately
your memory's been coming around

no longer numb
the heart starts to feel
the wounds of the past
so vivid and real

i can't help but to wonder
is moving on as easy as you make it seem?
or in the stillness of the night
does the past haunt you like it haunts me?

rock bottom of grief.

that makes two hundred and sixty-three
all these nights i can't sleep, can't breathe
keep getting caught up
just trying to catch some peace
praying like hell on my knees
with the bottle to my lips
because the pain never leaves

my head knows it'll get better
but my heart doesn't believe

i think it's safe to say
this is the rock bottom of grief

unpack.

they say what goes around comes around
but you left and never looked back

words left unsaid, feelings left unpacked
four years later, still wondering where you're at
guess there's no such thing as
"no strings attached"

no. 2072.

been 196 weeks since the last time you held me
crazy how time flies with or without an apology

makin' cowboys cry.

in the wild west
where the sun sets high
where the outlaws hide and the cowboys ride
lay an old gypsy soul under a western sky
echos of you saying *i can't get you off my mind*
but i can't stay and you wonder *why?*
i'm no good at love
only goodbye
and makin' cowboys cry

distractions.

i was dizzy on division
when you saw me kissing him
is that what it takes to get you listening?

i was fighting demons on demonbreun
playing hard to get while gettin' some
yeah, but it's time to face the truth

ain't nobody ever make me feel the way you did
seeing someone new doesn't make me forget
thought i'd move on by now but God forbid
been six years and i still can't quit

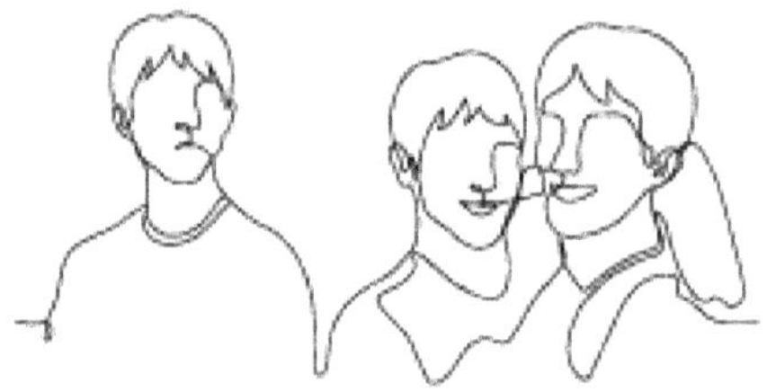

headaches and hangovers.

bound to die one day from these damn cigarettes
or getting blitzed just trying to forget
how i feel when i'm holding you
and a bottle of booze

i quit trying to quit
cause there's nothing i can do
i can't shake this headache from being hungover
or this heartache from being hung up on you

liminal.

i peeked over the fence
as you teetered on the edge
haunted by whispers that danced in your head

now you wrestle your demons
in the dead of the night
while i lay awake thinking
you are the high i'll chase for the rest of my life

still yearning for truths we both chose to hide
as you drown in your doubts
and i suffocate in my pride

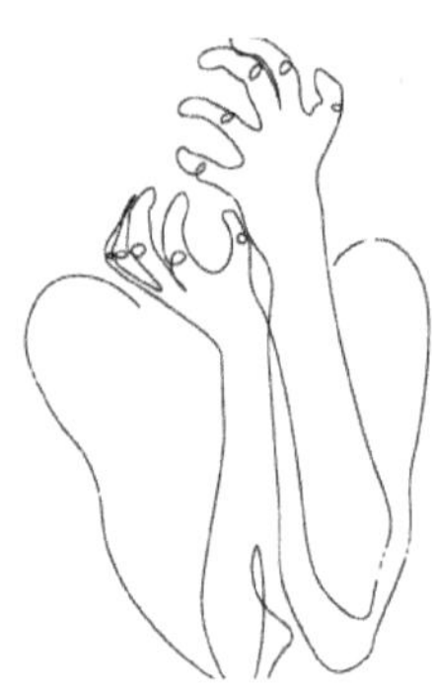

tennessee.

it's do or die
wrong or right
let go or hang tight
and i don't want to be the only one hoping
we're in each other's arms tomorrow morning

i know this fire could
burn for the rest of our lives
i'd do anything to make you mine
give it a shot and you'll see
you make the call, honey
what's it gonna be?
please stay with me in tennessee

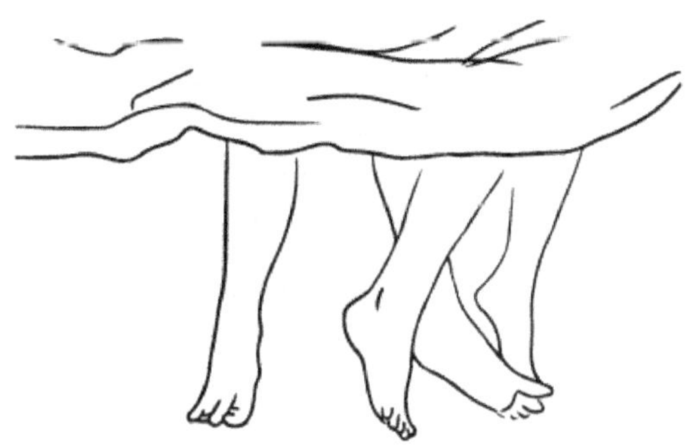

labyrinth.

an unbreakable bond experienced by many
but discussed by few
there's just something about growing together
while drifting apart too

a soul tie, perhaps, for they understood you
as much as you understood yourself
you'll spend years trying to outrun
all the feelings undeniably felt

while loss is clear cut… grief is anything but.

loving you, losing me.

i'm settled in and so happy with you
but finding my calling is long overdue
behind the mask, i hide
my tongue twisted and
locked with a makeshift lid & lies
the words are anchored down
there is no sound
my mouth won't move
i can't communicate what i'm trying to prove
my hands are tied
the motions i can't find
my body won't stop shaking
i can't sit still to tell you
my heart just keeps breaking
it'll be in pieces until i find my purpose
aside from loving you, my path seems searchless

but at least i have you if nothing else—
i just hate loving you more than i love myself

eleven twenty seven.

your hands viciously around my neck
i try so hard to stop the train before the wreck
but sometimes when you slam on the breaks
it's a little too late
you can't escape the devil
if you've already accepted his bait
i can't scream, i can't move, and i can't win
you slam my head against the wall
until it caves in
i try to fight back but i'm so confused
did you really just use booze as an excuse?
it doesn't matter if you aren't sober
anyway—
the sun's creeping in now...
i guess my birthday is over

drowning.

surrounded by these walls
but i don't think they're mine
tossing and turning
what ifs keeping me up all night
you got me lost inside a maze of my own mind
it's so like me to love someone
who doesn't treat me right
i wait for you to come around
losing my voice while you don't make a sound
i'm in the deep end, don't let me drown
my lungs are full but I feel nothing now

dissected.

the only way i know how to process loss
is to write from the heart
uncensored and raw
ripping the memories apart
dissecting past conversations and calling it art

so many memories that can never be erased
my mind distracted
but brought back by the ghost of your embrace
all the words i never said
provoke a bittersweet taste
been asking God *why this is the reality we face?*
so much love left to give
now it goes to waste

young love.

to know you is to love you
in a different time and another place
so until i see you again at the heavenly gates
i hope you're dancing in the sky
and singing in space

comic relief.

his paws unsteady
knees weak
denim is petty
he's cryin' like, *"pet me already!"*
hearts heavy
he's jelly but on the surface
he looks calm and ready
to find mom
cause he keeps on upsetting lola
provoked now, the whole pound howls so loud
he opens his mouth
but the barks won't come out
yeah, he's poutin' now
others getting scratches, *how?!*
times up, *"ruff"* & *"howl"*

soundproof.

they say love will come
when you're not looking
you said to hell with it
"i've already been broken"
ain't a girl in the world
that could change your mind
you were dead set on leaving love behind
even if it came knocking one day
you said you wouldn't hear
built your walls soundproof
so you could *"focus on your career"*

happy hits different.

never had anyone protect me the way you do
no one else that i was ever scared to lose
not a thing in this world
could make me more sure

happy just hits different with you

radio silence.

your silence is so fucking loud
i try to forget but i don't know how

can't forgive cause i'm too damn proud
stubborn as hell and my demons surmount

everyone knows *"busy"* is just an excuse
you swore you were different
just like they always do

but i can still hear your silence from the moon

phantom feelings.

i thought i held our fragile world
so carefully in my trembling hands
but love was never meant to be
a burden carried alone—
and at the time I failed to understand

i was the one who stitched the seams
whispered promises into the cracks
and called it whole
even when it wasn't what it seemed

i gave and kept giving
until giving became the only language i knew
while you forgot how to speak it back
and slowly withdrew

still, i loved you more fiercely
than anyone i've ever known
even as my spirit unraveled
when the weight of us
grew too heavy for my heart to bear alone…

and God,
even now
even in the quiet ache of letting go

the echo of you
still feels like home